Water Scarcity Diplomacy: Addressing the Challenges in the Nile River Basin

Copyright Page

TITLE: Water Scarcity Diplomacy: Addressing the Challenges in he Nile River Basin

1ST Edition

Copyright @ 2023

Roberto M. Rodriguez. All rights reserved.

ISBN: 9798223852643

Table of Contents

Water Scarcity Diplomacy: Addressing Challenges in the Nile River Basin

By Roberto Miguel Rodriguez

Chapter 1: The precious water of the Nile River: Disputes, Challenges, and Potential Solutions

Disputes over Nile River water allocation

The Nile River, often referred to as the lifeblood of Africa, has been a source of both unity and contention among the countries that it traverses. As diplomats, it is crucial to understand the historical and ongoing disputes over the allocation of Nile River water resources in order to address the challenges and find potential solutions.

The precious water of the Nile River holds immense value for the countries along its course, and the disputes over its allocation stem from the varying needs and interests of these nations. Egypt, for instance, heavily relies on the Nile River for agriculture, drinking water, and electricity generation. Ethiopia, on the other hand, seeks to harness the river's potential through the construction of the Grand Ethiopian Renaissance Dam (GERD) to meet its growing energy demands.

These contrasting interests have led to a complex web of hydropolitics, with countries negotiating and competing for their fair share of the Nile River water resources. International organizations such as the Nile Basin Initiative (NBI) and the United Nations have played a pivotal role in facilitating dialogue and resolving disputes among the riparian states.

However, the challenges go beyond mere disagreements over water allocation. Climate change has emerged as a critical factor affecting the availability of Nile River water. Rising temperatures, changing rainfall patterns, and increased evaporation rates are all impacting the river's flow and exacerbating water scarcity in the Nile River basin.

Furthermore, population growth and rapid urbanization have placed additional strain on the demand for Nile River water. As the population continues to surge, the need for water for drinking, sanitation, and agriculture has intensified, necessitating effective water management strategies and innovative technologies to ensure sustainability.

Agricultural challenges also pose a significant concern in the Nile River basin. The inefficient use of water, outdated irrigation techniques, and limited access to modern technologies have hindered agricultural productivity and exacerbated water scarcity. Implementing water management strategies such as drip irrigation and promoting water-saving practices can help address these challenges.

Moreover, urbanization has led to increased water pollution in the Nile River. Industrial effluents, untreated sewage, and solid waste discharge have polluted the river, threatening both human health and aquatic ecosystems. Mitigation measures such as improved wastewater treatment and stricter regulations are crucial to safeguard the Nile River's water quality.

The role of dams and reservoirs cannot be overlooked in managing Nile River water resources. These infrastructure projects offer opportunities for hydropower generation, flood control, and water storage. However, their construction must be carried out in a manner that considers the interests and concerns of all riparian states, ensuring equitable benefits and minimal ecological impact.

Lastly, indigenous communities' perspectives on the use and conservation of Nile River water must be incorporated into water scarcity diplomacy. Their traditional knowledge and sustainable practices can offer valuable insights for achieving a balance between water utilization and conservation.

In conclusion, the disputes over Nile River water allocation are multifaceted and require comprehensive understanding and diplomatic efforts. By addressing the historical and ongoing challenges, exploring potential solutions, and incorporating various perspectives, diplomats can pave the way for sustainable management of the precious water resources in the Nile River basin.

Historical context of Nile River water disputes

The Nile River, often referred to as the lifeblood of northeastern Africa, has been at the center of numerous historical disputes over water allocation. Understanding the historical context of these disputes is crucial in addressing the challenges faced in the Nile River Basin today.

The allocation of Nile River water resources has been a contentious issue for centuries. The river passes through eleven countries, each with its own water demands and development priorities. The historical disputes can be traced back to colonial times when the British Empire, as the colonizing power, exerted control over the river's resources. The 1929 and 1959 Nile River Agreements between Egypt and Sudan further exacerbated tensions, as they significantly favored Egypt's water rights, leaving downstream countries at a disadvantage.

Over the years, population growth, agricultural expansion, and urbanization have intensified the demand for Nile River water. This has led to an increased number of conflicts and disagreements among riparian countries. The construction of dams and reservoirs by upstream countries, such as Ethiopia's Grand Ethiopian Renaissance Dam, has further complicated the situation, as downstream countries fear potential disruptions to their water supply.

Hydropolitics and the role of international organizations have played a significant role in resolving Nile River water disputes. Regional organizations like the Nile Basin Initiative (NBI) have been established to promote cooperation and dialogue among riparian countries. International organizations, such as the United Nations and the World Bank, have also been involved in mediating conflicts and facilitating negotiations.

Indigenous communities in the Nile River Basin have their own perspectives on the use and conservation of water resources. Their traditional knowledge and practices can provide valuable insights into sustainable water management strategies.

In recent years, innovative technologies and approaches have emerged as potential solutions for sustainable management of Nile River water. These include water recycling, desalination, and drip irrigation systems, which can help mitigate water scarcity and increase efficiency.

To address the challenges posed by water scarcity in the Nile River Basin, it is crucial for diplomats and policymakers to understand the historical context of water disputes. By considering the causes and effects of water scarcity, the impact of climate change, and the perspectives of indigenous communities, sustainable solutions can be developed. Effective water management strategies, supported by international cooperation and the use of innovative technologies, will be key in ensuring the equitable allocation and conservation of the precious water resources of the Nile River.

International legal frameworks for resolving Nile River water disputes

The Nile River, known as the lifeblood of Africa, has long been a source of disputes and challenges among the countries sharing its waters. Resolving these disputes requires a comprehensive understanding of the international legal frameworks that govern the allocation and management of the Nile River's water resources. This subchapter aims to provide diplomats with an overview of these frameworks and their potential role in resolving Nile River water disputes.

One of the key international legal frameworks relevant to Nile River water disputes is the 1959 Nile Waters Agreement. This agreement, signed between Egypt and Sudan, divided the Nile River's waters between the two countries, leaving no allocated share for the other riparian states. This agreement has been a source of contention and has sparked calls for its revision to ensure a more equitable distribution of water resources among all Nile Basin countries.

Another significant legal framework is the United Nations Convention on the Law of the Non-Navigational Uses of International Watercourses. This convention, adopted in 1997, provides a comprehensive legal framework for the utilization, conservation, and protection of international watercourses. While not specifically tailored to the Nile River, it offers important principles and guidelines that can inform the resolution of disputes among Nile Basin countries.

The Nile Basin Initiative (NBI) is another important mechanism for resolving water disputes in the region. The NBI, established in 1999, aims to promote cooperation among Nile Basin countries in the sustainable management, utilization, and development of the Nile River's water resources. It provides a platform for dialogue and negotiation, facilitating the development of mutually beneficial agreements and frameworks.

In addition to these specific legal frameworks, there are a number of international organizations that play a crucial role in resolving Nile River water disputes. Organizations such as the African Union, the United Nations, and the World Bank provide technical support, mediation, and financing for cooperative water management initiatives in the Nile Basin.

Resolving Nile River water disputes requires a combination of legal frameworks, diplomatic negotiations, and technical expertise. By understanding and utilizing the existing international legal frameworks and collaborating with relevant international organizations, diplomats can contribute to the sustainable and equitable management of the Nile River's precious water resources.

Potential solutions for equitable Nile River water allocation

Water scarcity in the Nile River basin is a pressing issue that requires careful consideration and effective solutions. As diplomats, it is crucial to address the challenges faced in allocating Nile River water resources in an equitable manner. This subchapter explores potential solutions that can contribute to the sustainable management of the Nile River water for all stakeholders involved.

One potential solution is the establishment of a cooperative framework among the Nile River basin countries. This framework could facilitate dialogue, negotiation, and cooperation in the allocation and management of the Nile River water resources. It would be essential for diplomats to promote trust-building measures and facilitate open discussions to address historical disputes and ensure a fair distribution of water.

Another solution lies in the implementation of advanced technologies for water management. This includes the use of precision irrigation techniques, water-efficient agricultural practices, and innovative water storage and distribution systems. By adopting these technologies, countries can optimize water usage and reduce wastage, thereby promoting equitable allocation of Nile River water resources.

Furthermore, the involvement of international organizations such as the United Nations, the African Union, and the World Bank can play a significant role in resolving water disputes. These organizations can provide technical expertise, financial support, and mediation services to facilitate negotiations and ensure fair water allocation.

Additionally, it is essential to consider the impact of climate change on the availability of Nile River water. Diplomats should advocate for climate change adaptation strategies, such as the development of early warning systems, climate-resilient infrastructure, and sustainable land management practices. These measures can help mitigate the adverse effects of climate change on water availability and ensure equitable allocation of water resources.

Lastly, the inclusion of indigenous communities' perspectives in water management decisions is crucial. Diplomats should engage with these communities, learn from their traditional knowledge, and involve them in decision-making processes. This will not only promote equity but also foster sustainable water management practices that are harmonious with the cultural and ecological values of the Nile River.

In conclusion, addressing the challenges of equitable Nile River water allocation requires a comprehensive and collaborative approach. By establishing a cooperative framework, adopting advanced technologies, involving international organizations, considering climate change impacts, and including indigenous perspectives, diplomats can contribute to the sustainable management of the Nile River water resources and ensure a fair distribution for all stakeholders.

Chapter 2: Water scarcity in the Nile River basin: Causes and effects

Factors contributing to water scarcity in the Nile River basin

Water scarcity in the Nile River basin is a complex issue that is influenced by multiple factors. Understanding these factors is crucial for diplomats and other stakeholders in order to address the challenges and find potential solutions. This subchapter aims to explore the various factors contributing to water scarcity in the Nile River basin.

One of the primary factors is the impact of climate change on the availability of Nile River water. Climate change has led to increased temperatures, altered rainfall patterns, and rising sea levels, all of which have significant implications for water resources in the basin. Diplomats need to be aware of these changes and work towards implementing adaptive strategies to mitigate the effects of climate change on water availability.

Historical and ongoing disputes over the allocation of Nile River water resources also contribute to water scarcity in the basin. The Nile River is shared by multiple countries, and disagreements over water rights and usage have been a source of tension for decades. Effective diplomatic negotiations and the involvement of international organizations are necessary to find equitable and sustainable solutions to these disputes.

The impact of population growth on the demand for Nile River water cannot be ignored. The population in the Nile River basin is rapidly increasing, leading to increased water consumption for domestic, agricultural, and industrial purposes. Diplomats must consider the implications of population growth and work towards implementing efficient water management strategies to meet the growing demand.

Agricultural challenges are another significant factor contributing to water scarcity in the Nile River basin. Agriculture accounts for a substantial portion of water consumption in the basin, and inefficient irrigation practices exacerbate water scarcity. Implementing sustainable agricultural practices and improving water management techniques are crucial steps in addressing this issue.

Urbanization and water pollution are also contributing factors to water scarcity in the Nile River. Rapid urbanization leads to increased demand for water, while inadequate infrastructure and poor waste management practices result in water pollution. Diplomats need to focus on implementing effective pollution control measures and promoting sustainable urban development to mitigate the impact on water resources.

The construction of dams and reservoirs has both positive and negative impacts on water availability in the Nile River basin. While these infrastructure projects can provide hydroelectric power generation and water storage, they can also disrupt the natural flow of the river and affect downstream water availability. Diplomats should consider the benefits and drawbacks of dam construction and reservoir management to ensure sustainable water resource management in the basin.

Lastly, indigenous communities' perspectives on the use and conservation of Nile River water should be taken into account. These communities have a deep understanding of the river's ecology and can provide valuable insights into sustainable water management practices. Diplomats should engage with indigenous communities and incorporate their perspectives into decision-making processes.

In conclusion, water scarcity in the Nile River basin is influenced by a multitude of factors. Diplomats need to consider the impact of climate change, historical disputes, population growth, agricultural challenges, urbanization, pollution, dam construction, and indigenous perspectives in order to develop effective strategies for sustainable water management. By addressing these factors, diplomats can contribute to resolving water scarcity challenges in the Nile River basin and promote cooperation among riparian countries.

Impacts of water scarcity on communities and ecosystems

Water scarcity is a pressing issue that affects communities and ecosystems in the Nile River Basin and requires the attention of diplomats and other stakeholders. This subchapter aims to shed light on the various impacts of water scarcity on these vital aspects of life.

Communities residing in the Nile River Basin heavily rely on its waters for drinking, sanitation, and agricultural purposes. However, as water scarcity intensifies, these communities face numerous challenges. Limited access to clean water can lead to a rise in waterborne diseases and malnutrition, particularly affecting vulnerable populations such as women and children. Moreover, conflicts over water resources can arise, exacerbating existing political tensions and potentially leading to social unrest. Therefore, diplomats must understand the far-reaching implications of water scarcity on communities to effectively address this issue.

In addition to the human impacts, water scarcity also poses a threat to the delicate ecosystems of the Nile River Basin. Reduced water flows and altered water quality can disrupt aquatic habitats and harm biodiversity. Fish populations, for instance, may decline, affecting both subsistence and commercial fisheries. Furthermore, the degradation of ecosystems can lead to a loss of ecosystem services, including water purification and flood regulation, which are essential for sustainable development. Diplomats must recognize the interconnectedness between communities and ecosystems and strive for solutions that prioritize the preservation of both.

The impacts of climate change further compound the challenges of water scarcity in the Nile River Basin. Rising temperatures, changing rainfall patterns, and increased evaporation rates pose significant threats to water availability. Diplomats should acknowledge the need for proactive measures to adapt to these changing conditions and work towards sustainable water management strategies.

To address water scarcity diplomatically, international organizations and cooperation play a crucial role. By facilitating dialogue, fostering agreements, and sharing best practices, these organizations can help resolve disputes over the allocation of Nile River water resources. Effective hydropolitics and collaboration can lead to equitable and sustainable solutions that benefit all stakeholders.

In conclusion, water scarcity in the Nile River Basin has far-reaching impacts on communities and ecosystems. Diplomats must recognize the urgency and complexity of this issue to address the challenges effectively. By prioritizing inclusivity, cooperation, and sustainable management practices, they can work towards ensuring the availability of water resources for present and future generations.

Economic consequences of water scarcity in the Nile River basin

Water scarcity is an increasingly pressing challenge in the Nile River basin, with significant economic consequences that demand the attention of diplomats and various stakeholders. This subchapter explores the intricate relationship between water scarcity and its economic impacts in the region, shedding light on the urgency of addressing this issue.

The Nile River, often referred to as the lifeblood of the region, plays a vital role in supporting various economic activities. Agriculture, for instance, heavily relies on the river's water for irrigation, contributing to food security and livelihoods. However, as water scarcity intensifies, the availability of water for irrigation diminishes, directly impacting agricultural productivity. This, in turn, results in reduced crop yields, decreased incomes for farmers, and a rise in food prices, leading to increased poverty levels and exacerbating socio-economic inequalities.

Furthermore, the Nile River basin is home to rapidly growing urban centers, which exert additional pressure on water resources. The increasing demand for water in urban areas, coupled with inadequate infrastructure and pollution, poses significant challenges for water management. As a consequence, industries reliant on water, such as manufacturing and tourism, face uncertainties and potential disruptions, leading to decreased investments, job losses, and a decline in economic growth.

Climate change exacerbates the already precarious water scarcity situation in the Nile River basin. Rising temperatures and changing rainfall patterns directly affect the availability of water resources, exacerbating competition and increasing the risk of conflicts over water allocation. Diplomats play a crucial role in addressing these challenges by facilitating dialogue and cooperation among riparian countries to develop sustainable water management strategies.

International organizations also have a vital role to play in resolving Nile River water disputes. Their involvement can promote equitable and inclusive agreements, ensure the efficient allocation of water resources, and support the implementation of innovative technologies and approaches for sustainable water management.

To mitigate the economic consequences of water scarcity, various measures can be taken. These include investing in water-efficient irrigation techniques, promoting water recycling and reuse, implementing water pricing mechanisms to incentivize conservation, and fostering international cooperation to develop and implement joint projects for water resource management.

In conclusion, water scarcity in the Nile River basin has far-reaching economic consequences that demand the attention and collaboration of diplomats and stakeholders. By understanding the causes and effects of water scarcity, promoting sustainable water management strategies, and engaging in meaningful dialogue, it is possible to mitigate the economic impacts and ensure the continued prosperity of the region.

Social and political implications of water scarcity in the region

Water scarcity has become a pressing issue in the Nile River basin, with far-reaching social and political implications. As diplomats, it is crucial to understand the multifaceted nature of this problem and explore potential solutions that can address the challenges faced by the region.

The precious water of the Nile River has been a source of disputes, challenges, and potential solutions. The limited availability of water resources has led to tensions between riparian states, as each seeks to secure its share of this vital resource. Historical and ongoing disputes over the allocation of Nile River water resources have strained diplomatic relations and necessitate a coordinated effort to find equitable solutions.

Moreover, climate change exacerbates the availability of Nile River water, with rising temperatures and changing precipitation patterns. This poses a significant threat to the region's water security, further compounding the challenges faced by diplomats. It is imperative to acknowledge the impact of climate change and develop adaptive measures to mitigate its effects.

Agricultural challenges and water management strategies are also central to addressing water scarcity in the region. Population growth intensifies the demand for Nile River water, particularly for agricultural purposes. Diplomats must engage in dialogue and cooperation to implement sustainable water management strategies that balance the needs of agriculture and the environment.

Urbanization and water pollution pose additional challenges in the Nile River basin. Rapid urban growth increases the strain on water resources and exacerbates pollution levels, affecting both human health and ecosystem integrity. Diplomats must prioritize the development and implementation of effective mitigation measures to address these issues and protect the water quality of the Nile River.

The role of dams and reservoirs in managing Nile River water resources cannot be overlooked. While these infrastructures can provide opportunities for water storage and hydropower generation, their construction and operation can impact downstream countries' water availability. Diplomatic efforts should focus on ensuring equitable and sustainable dam operations that consider the needs of all riparian states.

Indigenous communities' perspectives on the use and conservation of Nile River water are crucial in shaping effective water management policies. Diplomats must engage with these communities, respecting their rights and traditional knowledge, to develop inclusive and sustainable approaches to water scarcity.

Finally, innovative technologies and approaches can play a significant role in the sustainable management of Nile River water. From efficient irrigation systems to water recycling and desalination, diplomats should explore and support the adoption of these technologies to alleviate water scarcity in the region.

In conclusion, water scarcity in the Nile River basin brings forth social and political implications that demand diplomatic attention. By understanding the causes and effects of water scarcity, engaging in hydropolitics, and collaborating with international organizations, diplomats can work towards resolving disputes, implementing sustainable management strategies, and ensuring the equitable distribution of Nile River water resources.

Chapter 3: The impact of climate change on the availability of Nile River water

Climate change projections for the Nile River basin

As diplomats, it is crucial to understand the potential impacts of climate change on the Nile River basin, one of the world's most vital water resources. The Nile River sustains the livelihoods of millions of people across several countries, making it a topic of significant concern and discussion. This subchapter aims to provide you with insights into the climate change projections for the Nile River basin, equipping you with essential knowledge to address water scarcity diplomatically.

Climate change is projected to have severe consequences on the availability and distribution of water in the Nile River basin. Scientific research indicates that rising temperatures and changing precipitation patterns will lead to increased evaporation rates, causing a reduction in overall water availability. Moreover, climate models predict an increase in the frequency and intensity of droughts, exacerbating water scarcity issues in the region.

Another challenge posed by climate change is the potential for increased variability in the river's flow. With changing rainfall patterns, the Nile River basin may experience more extreme floods and periods of low flow, affecting water availability for irrigation, hydropower generation, and domestic use. Such variability will require adaptive water management strategies to ensure sustainable and equitable water allocation.

Furthermore, rising temperatures are expected to accelerate glacial melt in the mountains that feed the Nile River, leading to increased water flow initially but ultimately jeopardizing the long-term water supply. Additionally, sea-level rise due to climate change may result in saltwater intrusion into the Nile Delta, contaminating freshwater resources and affecting agriculture and aquaculture.

Addressing these climate change impacts requires a collaborative approach among Nile River basin countries. Diplomatic efforts should focus on strengthening regional cooperation, sharing data, and developing joint adaptation strategies. International organizations, such as the Nile Basin Initiative, can play a vital role in facilitating dialogue and resolving disputes over water allocation.

In conclusion, understanding the climate change projections for the Nile River basin is essential for diplomats seeking to address water scarcity diplomatically. By recognizing the potential challenges and taking proactive measures, we can mitigate the adverse impacts of climate change on the availability and distribution of Nile River water. Through diplomatic negotiations and cooperation, we can ensure the sustainable management of this precious resource for the benefit of present and future generations.

Effects of climate change on water availability in the region

Climate change is a pressing issue that has far-reaching implications for water availability in the Nile River basin. As diplomats, it is crucial to understand the potential effects of climate change on this precious resource and the challenges it poses for the region.

One of the most significant impacts of climate change is the alteration of precipitation patterns. As temperatures rise, the region may experience more frequent and intense droughts, leading to reduced water availability in the Nile River. This will have severe consequences for the agricultural sector, as irrigation demands will surpass the available water supply. Diplomats must recognize the potential for increased tensions and conflicts over water allocation as a result of these changes.

Furthermore, rising temperatures could accelerate the melting of glaciers and snowpack in the region's mountains. This will initially increase water availability, but in the long term, it will lead to reduced water supply as these natural reservoirs diminish. Diplomatic efforts should focus on the development of sustainable water management strategies that account for these changes and ensure equitable distribution among all countries sharing the Nile River.

Another concern is the potential increase in extreme weather events, such as floods and storms. These events can cause significant damage to water infrastructure, leading to disruptions in the supply of clean water. Diplomats must address the need for resilient infrastructure that can withstand these events and ensure the continued availability of water for communities in the region.

Climate change also exacerbates existing water pollution challenges in the Nile River. Rising temperatures can increase the growth of harmful algal blooms and pathogens, posing risks to both human health and ecosystems. Diplomatic efforts should prioritize the development and implementation of mitigation measures to reduce pollution and protect the quality of water in the Nile River.

In conclusion, climate change poses significant challenges to water availability in the Nile River basin. As diplomats, it is essential to recognize these effects and work towards sustainable and equitable water management strategies. By addressing the impacts of climate change on water availability, we can contribute to the resolution of disputes, protection of water resources, and the overall well-being of the region.

Adaptation strategies to mitigate the impact of climate change on Nile River water resources

As diplomats, it is crucial to be well-informed about the challenges facing the Nile River basin, particularly with regards to water scarcity and the impact of climate change. In this subchapter, we will explore various adaptation strategies that can be employed to mitigate the effects of climate change on Nile River water resources.

Climate change poses a significant threat to the availability of Nile River water, as rising temperatures and changing precipitation patterns can lead to increased evaporation and reduced water supply. To address this, it is essential to implement adaptive measures that promote sustainable water management and enhance resilience in the face of climate uncertainties.

One key strategy is the promotion of water conservation and efficient use. This can be achieved through the implementation of water-saving technologies, such as drip irrigation and precision agriculture. By reducing water wastage and optimizing irrigation practices, countries in the Nile River basin can ensure the availability of water resources for both agricultural and domestic purposes.

Another important adaptation strategy is the development of climate-resilient infrastructure, such as dams and reservoirs. These structures can help regulate water flow, store excess water during periods of high precipitation, and release it during dry spells. Additionally, they can provide opportunities for hydropower generation, contributing to both water and energy security in the region.

International cooperation and the involvement of relevant organizations are crucial in resolving disputes over Nile River water resources. By fostering dialogue and collaboration, diplomats can facilitate the development of equitable and sustainable water-sharing agreements that take into account the impacts of climate change.

Furthermore, it is essential to consider the perspectives of indigenous communities who have traditionally relied on the Nile River for their livelihoods. Their knowledge and practices in water use and conservation should be acknowledged and integrated into adaptation strategies. This can help ensure the preservation of cultural heritage while promoting sustainable water management approaches.

Lastly, the exploration of innovative technologies and approaches is paramount in achieving sustainable management of Nile River water. This may include the utilization of desalination techniques, rainwater harvesting, and the implementation of smart water management systems. These innovative solutions can help optimize water use, reduce losses, and enhance the overall resilience of the Nile River basin in the face of climate change.

In conclusion, adapting to the impacts of climate change on Nile River water resources requires a comprehensive approach that combines water conservation, climate-resilient infrastructure, international cooperation, indigenous knowledge, and innovative technologies. By implementing these adaptation strategies, diplomats can contribute to the sustainable management of the precious water of the Nile River and ensure its availability for future generations.

Chapter 4: Historical and ongoing disputes over the allocation of Nile River water resources

Historical conflicts and negotiations over Nile River water allocation

Water scarcity diplomacy has been a critical issue in the Nile River Basin for centuries, as numerous historical conflicts and negotiations have revolved around the allocation of its precious water resources. This subchapter delves into the intricate web of disputes, challenges, and potential solutions that have shaped the region's water landscape.

The Nile River, spanning over eleven countries, has long been a source of contention due to its vital role in sustaining livelihoods, agriculture, and economic development. Historical conflicts have arisen primarily between upstream and downstream countries, each vying for a fair share of the river's waters. These disputes have often escalated into diplomatic tensions, necessitating negotiations to address the complexities surrounding water allocation.

Hydropolitics, the nexus between water resources and politics, has played a significant role in these conflicts. International organizations, such as the Nile Basin Initiative, have attempted to mediate and facilitate negotiations between the riparian states, recognizing the need for collective action to ensure equitable water distribution. The subchapter explores the role and effectiveness of these organizations in resolving Nile River water disputes.

Furthermore, population growth and increasing urbanization have exacerbated the demand for Nile River water. As the population continues to grow, agricultural challenges have emerged, prompting the need for effective water management strategies. The subchapter highlights the implications of population growth on water demand and explores potential solutions to meet the increasing needs sustainably.

The impact of climate change on the availability of Nile River water cannot be ignored. As temperatures rise and rainfall patterns become unpredictable, the subchapter delves into the potential consequences of climate change on the region's water resources. It also explores the need for adaptation measures to ensure water security in the face of a changing climate.

Additionally, the subchapter touches upon the perspectives of indigenous communities on the use and conservation of Nile River water. Their traditional knowledge and practices offer valuable insights into sustainable water management and conservation efforts.

Finally, the subchapter discusses innovative technologies and approaches that can contribute to the sustainable management of Nile River water. From water recycling and desalination technologies to integrated water resource management, these solutions hold promise in addressing the challenges posed by water scarcity in the basin.

In conclusion, historical conflicts and negotiations over Nile River water allocation have shaped the region's water scarcity diplomacy. By understanding the causes and effects of these conflicts, exploring potential solutions, and considering the perspectives of various stakeholders, diplomats can play a crucial role in promoting sustainable water management and securing the future of the Nile River Basin.

Current disputes and challenges in managing Nile River water resources

The Nile River, with its abundant waters, has been a source of life and sustenance for the countries in the Nile River Basin. However, the management of these precious water resources has been marred by disputes and challenges that require urgent attention and diplomatic efforts. This subchapter discusses the current disputes and challenges in managing Nile River water resources and explores potential solutions.

One of the major issues in the Nile River Basin is the historical and ongoing disputes over the allocation of water resources. The Nile River flows through eleven countries, each with its own demands and priorities. This has led to conflicts over the fair distribution of water, especially between upstream and downstream countries. Diplomatic efforts are needed to find a consensus and establish a fair and equitable water-sharing agreement that takes into account the needs and rights of all countries involved.

Another challenge is the impact of climate change on the availability of Nile River water. Changing weather patterns, increased temperatures, and unpredictable rainfall have affected the flow of the river. As a result, water scarcity has become a pressing issue in the basin, exacerbating existing tensions. Diplomats must address this challenge by promoting sustainable water management practices, encouraging the use of water-saving technologies, and supporting climate change adaptation measures.

The demand for Nile River water is also increasing due to population growth and urbanization. Rapid population growth in the region has put additional pressure on water resources, particularly for agricultural and domestic use. Diplomats must work towards finding innovative solutions to meet the growing demand, such as promoting water-efficient agricultural practices and implementing water conservation measures in urban areas.

Furthermore, the construction of dams and reservoirs along the Nile River has added another layer of complexity to water management. While these structures provide benefits like hydroelectric power and irrigation, they also have implications for downstream countries and the environment. Diplomats need to facilitate dialogue and cooperation between countries to ensure that the construction and operation of dams are done in a way that minimizes negative impacts and maximizes shared benefits.

Lastly, the subchapter explores the role of international organizations in resolving Nile River water disputes. Organizations such as the Nile Basin Initiative and the United Nations have played a crucial role in promoting dialogue, cooperation, and conflict resolution among the riparian countries. Diplomats must actively engage with these organizations and encourage their involvement in finding sustainable solutions to the challenges facing the Nile River Basin.

In conclusion, the management of Nile River water resources faces numerous disputes and challenges. Diplomatic efforts are vital in addressing these issues and finding sustainable solutions. By promoting dialogue, cooperation, and the use of innovative technologies, diplomats can help secure the future of the Nile River and ensure its waters continue to benefit all the countries in the basin.

Role of diplomatic efforts in resolving Nile River water disputes

The Nile River, known as the lifeline of Africa, has been at the center of numerous disputes and challenges related to its precious water resources. As diplomats, it is crucial to understand the role of diplomatic efforts in resolving these disputes and finding sustainable solutions for the Nile River basin.

Historically, disputes over the allocation of Nile River water resources have been a major concern for riparian countries. These disputes have often arisen due to competing interests, colonial-era agreements, and population growth. Diplomatic efforts play a vital role in bringing together these countries to negotiate and find mutually beneficial solutions.

One of the key aspects of diplomatic efforts is the involvement of international organizations. Organizations such as the United Nations, African Union, and the Nile Basin Initiative have facilitated dialogue and negotiation processes among riparian countries. These organizations provide a platform for diplomatic engagement, fostering trust, cooperation, and understanding among stakeholders.

The impact of climate change on the availability of Nile River water further complicates the situation. Diplomats must recognize the importance of addressing climate change as a shared challenge and work towards developing climate-resilient water management strategies. This requires collaboration and information-sharing among riparian countries, as well as seeking support from international organizations and climate change conventions.

Another crucial factor to consider is the role of dams and reservoirs in managing Nile River water resources. Diplomatic efforts should focus on promoting equitable and sustainable dam construction and operation, taking into account the concerns and interests of all riparian countries. This can be achieved through negotiation, transparency, and adherence to international water law principles.

Furthermore, diplomatic efforts should also incorporate the perspectives of indigenous communities in the use and conservation of Nile River water. These communities have a deep understanding of the river's ecological balance and can contribute valuable insights to sustainable water management practices. Involving them in decision-making processes can lead to more inclusive and effective solutions.

Lastly, diplomats should explore innovative technologies and approaches for sustainable water management in the Nile River basin. These can include water recycling, desalination, and efficient irrigation techniques. By promoting the adoption of such technologies, diplomats can address the challenges of water scarcity and ensure the long-term availability of Nile River water resources.

In conclusion, diplomatic efforts play a crucial role in resolving Nile River water disputes and addressing the challenges faced by the region. By fostering cooperation, facilitating dialogue, and incorporating diverse perspectives, diplomats can work towards finding sustainable solutions for the Nile River basin. It is through such efforts that we can ensure the equitable and responsible management of the precious water resources of the Nile River for the benefit of all riparian countries and their populations.

Chapter 5: Hydropolitics and the role of international organizations in resolving Nile River water disputes

Political dynamics and power struggles in Nile River water management

Water management in the Nile River basin is not only a matter of resource allocation, but also a complex web of political dynamics and power struggles. This subchapter aims to provide an in-depth analysis of the political challenges faced in managing the precious water of the Nile River, with a focus on the role of diplomats in addressing these issues.

The Nile River, known as the lifeblood of the region, traverses through 11 countries, making it a transboundary resource that necessitates cooperation and coordination. However, historical and ongoing disputes over the allocation of Nile River water resources have hindered effective management. This chapter delves into the root causes of these disputes, including historical claims and power imbalances, and explores potential solutions that diplomats can advocate for.

Hydropolitics, the politics of water resources, plays a pivotal role in shaping the management of the Nile River. International organizations, such as the Nile Basin Initiative, have been instrumental in mediating conflicts and fostering cooperation among riparian countries. This subchapter discusses the role of these organizations and explores the challenges they face in resolving Nile River water disputes.

Population growth and urbanization are exerting immense pressure on the availability of Nile River water. As the demand for water increases, there is a need for diplomats to address the impact of these factors on water scarcity and develop strategies to manage the limited resources effectively. Moreover, the implications of urbanization on water pollution in the Nile River are explored, along with potential mitigation measures that can be implemented.

The construction of dams and reservoirs in the Nile River basin has significant implications for water management. Diplomats play a crucial role in navigating the complexities surrounding dam projects, ensuring equitable distribution and minimizing adverse environmental and social impacts. This subchapter examines the role of diplomats in managing these projects and the challenges they face in balancing competing interests.

Indigenous communities have a unique perspective on the use and conservation of Nile River water. This subchapter highlights the importance of incorporating their perspectives in water management policies and explores potential avenues for collaboration between diplomats and indigenous communities.

Lastly, this subchapter introduces innovative technologies and approaches for sustainable management of Nile River water. Diplomats can play a pivotal role in advocating for the adoption of these technologies and facilitating knowledge sharing among riparian countries.

Overall, this subchapter seeks to provide diplomats with a comprehensive understanding of the political dynamics and power struggles in Nile River water management. By addressing these challenges, diplomats can contribute to the sustainable and equitable use of this precious resource for the benefit of all riparian countries.

The role of international organizations in facilitating water diplomacy in the region

Water scarcity in the Nile River basin is a complex issue that requires the involvement and cooperation of various stakeholders, including international organizations. These organizations play a crucial role in facilitating water diplomacy in the region, aiming to address the challenges and disputes related to the precious water resources of the Nile River.

One of the primary roles of international organizations is to act as mediators and facilitators in resolving conflicts and disputes over the allocation of Nile River water resources. These organizations provide a neutral platform for dialogue and negotiations between riparian countries, helping them to reach mutually beneficial agreements and establish frameworks for water management.

By bringing together diplomats from different countries, international organizations create opportunities for open and transparent discussions on water-related issues. They provide a space for sharing information, data, and scientific research, which is essential for making informed decisions and developing effective water management strategies.

International organizations also play a crucial role in raising awareness about the impact of climate change on the availability of Nile River water. They help diplomats understand the long-term implications of climate change on water resources and encourage them to take proactive measures to mitigate its effects.

Additionally, these organizations support capacity-building initiatives in the region, helping diplomats and other stakeholders develop the necessary skills and knowledge to address water scarcity challenges. They provide training programs, technical assistance, and funding opportunities to strengthen the institutional capacity of riparian countries in managing their water resources sustainably.

Furthermore, international organizations contribute to the development and implementation of innovative technologies and approaches for the sustainable management of Nile River water. They promote the use of advanced water management techniques, such as water recycling, desalination, and rainwater harvesting, to increase water availability and reduce waste.

In conclusion, international organizations play a crucial role in facilitating water diplomacy in the Nile River basin. Through mediation, information sharing, capacity-building, and technological advancements, these organizations help diplomats address disputes, manage water scarcity challenges, and work towards sustainable water management in the region. Their involvement is vital to ensure the equitable and efficient allocation of the precious water resources of the Nile River.

Case studies of successful international water agreements in the Nile River basin

In the complex realm of water scarcity diplomacy, the Nile River basin has been a focal point for countless disputes and challenges. However, amidst these conflicts, there have been notable success stories of international water agreements that have effectively addressed the issues at hand. This subchapter delves into several case studies that highlight successful collaborative efforts in the Nile River basin, providing valuable insights for diplomats and stakeholders involved in water diplomacy.

One such case study is the Nile Basin Initiative (NBI), established in 1999. It aimed to promote cooperation among the Nile riparian countries and foster sustainable development in the region. The NBI has facilitated the negotiation and implementation of various agreements, including the Nile Equatorial Lakes Subsidiary Action Program (NELSAP). This program has successfully promoted hydropower development, irrigation, and flood control measures, benefitting multiple countries in the basin.

Another noteworthy case study is the 2010 Cooperative Framework Agreement (CFA) signed by six Nile Basin countries, including Ethiopia,

Rwanda, Uganda, Tanzania, Kenya, and Burundi. This agreement replaced the outdated colonial-era agreements and emphasized equitable utilization of the Nile River water resources. The CFA established a framework for cooperation, water allocations, and dispute resolution mechanisms, reflecting a significant step forward in resolving historical disputes.

Furthermore, the Al-Salam Canal project between Egypt and Sudan is a prime example of successful bilateral cooperation in the Nile River basin. This project, facilitated by the Joint Technical Commission for Nile Waters, has allowed for the transfer of water from the Nile to reclaim vast areas of desert land for agricultural purposes. By effectively managing and utilizing shared water resources, both countries have achieved significant economic and social benefits.

These case studies demonstrate that successful international water agreements in the Nile River basin require a combination of political will, technical expertise, and inclusive participation. They highlight the importance of multilateral platforms, such as the NBI, in fostering dialogue and collaboration among riparian countries. Moreover, the case studies underscore the significance of updating outdated agreements to reflect the changing dynamics in the region and address historical injustices.

For diplomats seeking to address the challenges in the Nile River basin, these case studies offer valuable lessons. They emphasize the need for proactive engagement, long-term planning, and the inclusion of indigenous communities in decision-making processes. By drawing upon the experiences of successful agreements, diplomats can gain insights into effective strategies and approaches to foster cooperation, sustainability, and equitable water allocation in the Nile River basin.

Chapter 6: The impact of population growth on the demand for Nile River water

Population growth trends in the Nile River basin

The population growth in the Nile River basin is a significant factor impacting the availability and demand for water resources in the region. As diplomats, it is crucial to understand and address the challenges posed by this population growth in order to ensure sustainable water management and avoid potential conflicts.

The Nile River basin is home to more than 250 million people, making it one of the most densely populated regions in Africa. The population growth rate in the basin has been steadily increasing over the past few decades, and it is projected to continue rising in the coming years. This rapid population growth has placed immense pressure on the already limited water resources of the Nile River, leading to water scarcity and various socio-economic challenges.

The increasing demand for water resulting from population growth has primarily been driven by two main factors: agricultural expansion and urbanization. Agriculture is the dominant sector in the Nile River basin, and the growing population requires more food production. This has led to the expansion of irrigated agriculture, which consumes a significant amount of water from the river. Similarly, rapid urbanization in the basin has led to increased water demand for domestic and industrial purposes.

The consequences of population growth in the Nile River basin are far-reaching. Water scarcity has led to reduced agricultural productivity, food insecurity, and the displacement of indigenous communities who rely on the river for their livelihoods. Moreover, the strain on water resources has exacerbated existing disputes over water allocation between riparian countries, leading to diplomatic tensions.

Addressing this population growth challenge requires a holistic approach that combines sustainable water management strategies with social and economic development efforts. Diplomats can play a crucial role in facilitating dialogue and cooperation among riparian countries to ensure equitable access to water resources. International organizations can also support capacity-building initiatives and provide technical assistance to promote efficient water use and conservation practices.

Furthermore, innovative technologies and approaches can contribute to sustainable water management in the Nile River basin. This includes the implementation of water-saving irrigation techniques, the use of wastewater treatment and recycling systems, and the development of water storage infrastructure such as dams and reservoirs.

In conclusion, the population growth in the Nile River basin has had significant implications for water scarcity and resource management in the region. Diplomats have a vital role to play in addressing these challenges by fostering cooperation, promoting sustainable water practices, and finding equitable solutions to water allocation disputes. By understanding and addressing the impact of population growth, we can work towards ensuring the long-term availability and sustainability of the precious water resources of the Nile River.

Water demand projections and challenges for meeting future needs

As diplomats, it is crucial to understand the water demand projections and the challenges that lie ahead in meeting future water needs in the Nile River basin. The precious water of the Nile River is not only a source of life but also a cause of disputes, challenges, and potential solutions. Water scarcity in the Nile River basin is a pressing issue that requires immediate attention.

One of the major factors affecting water availability in the Nile River basin is climate change. The impact of climate change on the availability of Nile River water is significant, and it poses a threat to the region's water resources. Rising temperatures, changing rainfall patterns, and increased evaporation rates are all contributing to decreased water availability.

Historical and ongoing disputes over the allocation of Nile River water resources further complicate the situation. Various countries in the basin have conflicting interests and demands, leading to diplomatic tensions. Resolving these disputes requires hydropolitics and the involvement of international organizations to facilitate dialogue and find mutually beneficial solutions.

Population growth is another crucial factor that affects the demand for Nile River water. The increasing population puts additional pressure on the already limited water resources. As the population grows, so does the need for water for domestic, agricultural, and industrial purposes. It is essential to address these challenges and develop strategies to manage water demand effectively.

Agricultural challenges and water management strategies play a significant role in the sustainable use of Nile River water. Efficient irrigation techniques, crop selection, and water conservation practices are essential to ensure water availability for agriculture, which is a major consumer of water resources in the basin.

Urbanization and water pollution are also contributing to the water scarcity in the Nile River. Rapid urbanization leads to increased water demand, while inadequate infrastructure and improper waste management contribute to water pollution. Mitigation measures such as improving wastewater treatment, promoting water conservation in urban areas, and implementing pollution control measures are necessary to address these challenges.

Dams and reservoirs play a vital role in managing Nile River water resources. These infrastructure projects help regulate water flow, store water for future use, and generate electricity. However, their construction often leads to controversies and disputes between countries. Balancing the benefits and drawbacks of dam construction is crucial for sustainable water management.

Indigenous communities' perspectives on the use and conservation of Nile River water should also be considered. Traditional knowledge and practices can provide valuable insights into sustainable water management strategies.

Lastly, innovative technologies and approaches should be explored for the sustainable management of Nile River water. From desalination and water reuse to remote sensing and data analytics, these technologies can help optimize water use and mitigate the challenges posed by water scarcity.

In conclusion, addressing the water demand projections and challenges for meeting future needs in the Nile River basin requires a comprehensive understanding of the issues at hand. By considering the perspectives of different stakeholders and implementing sustainable water management strategies, diplomats can play a crucial role in resolving disputes and ensuring the availability of water resources for future generations.

Strategies for managing water demands amidst population growth in the region

In recent years, the Nile River basin has faced a significant challenge in managing its water demands amidst population growth. As the population continues to increase, the demand for water resources in the region also rises. This subchapter explores various strategies that can be implemented to effectively manage water demands in the face of population growth.

One key strategy is the promotion of water conservation and efficiency measures. Diplomats can play a crucial role in advocating for the adoption of water-saving technologies and practices. This includes encouraging the use of modern irrigation technologies, such as drip irrigation, which can significantly reduce water wastage in agricultural practices. Additionally, diplomats can promote awareness campaigns to educate the public about water conservation techniques and the importance of responsible water use.

Another strategy is the development and implementation of integrated water resources management (IWRM) plans. These plans aim to harmonize water allocation and use across different sectors, including agriculture, industry, and domestic consumption. Diplomats can facilitate discussions between countries sharing the Nile River basin to develop a coordinated approach to water management. This could involve establishing joint institutions or mechanisms for sharing information and coordinating water allocation decisions.

Furthermore, the subchapter will explore the potential of wastewater treatment and reuse as a strategy for managing water demands. Diplomats can highlight the importance of investing in wastewater treatment infrastructure to ensure the safe reuse of water for non-potable purposes. This can help alleviate the strain on freshwater resources and reduce the overall demand for Nile River water.

Additionally, the subchapter will discuss the importance of international cooperation in managing water demands. Diplomats can emphasize the need for countries sharing the Nile River basin to engage in dialogue and negotiation to reach mutually beneficial agreements on water allocation. International organizations, such as the United Nations and the African

Union, can play a crucial role in facilitating these discussions and providing technical assistance.

Overall, managing water demands amidst population growth in the Nile River basin requires a comprehensive approach that integrates water conservation measures, IWRM plans, wastewater treatment, and international cooperation. Through effective diplomacy and collaboration, the challenges posed by population growth can be addressed, ensuring the sustainable management of the precious water resources of the Nile River for future generations.

Chapter 7: Agricultural challenges and water management strategies in the Nile River basin

Importance of agriculture and irrigation in the Nile River basin

Agriculture has historically played a crucial role in the Nile River basin, and its importance continues to be of utmost significance in the present day. As diplomats, it is essential to understand the intricate relationship between agriculture, irrigation, and the Nile River basin, as it directly affects the livelihoods, economies, and stability of the riparian countries.

The Nile River basin is home to some of the world's most fertile lands, which have been cultivated for centuries, providing food security for millions of people. Agriculture in this region relies heavily on the availability of water, making irrigation systems vital for agricultural productivity. Irrigation allows for controlled water supply, enabling farmers to grow a variety of crops throughout the year, even in the dry seasons.

The Nile River, with its abundant water resources, has traditionally supported agriculture in the basin. The river's waters provide a lifeline to farmers, allowing them to grow crops such as wheat, rice, maize, and cotton. These crops are not only essential for domestic consumption but also contribute significantly to the economies of the riparian countries through export.

However, water scarcity in the Nile River basin poses a significant challenge to agriculture and food security. The increasing demand for water due to population growth, coupled with the impacts of climate change, has put immense pressure on the available water resources. Droughts, unpredictable rainfall patterns, and rising temperatures have led to reduced river flows and increased evaporation rates, affecting the availability of water for irrigation.

Efficient water management strategies and innovative irrigation techniques are therefore crucial to sustain agricultural productivity in the Nile River basin. Diplomats must recognize the importance of investing in irrigation infrastructure, including modernizing existing systems and promoting the use of efficient irrigation methods such as drip irrigation and precision farming. These techniques not only optimize water use but also promote sustainable agricultural practices, reducing the negative impacts on the environment.

Furthermore, international cooperation and the involvement of relevant international organizations are paramount in resolving disputes over the allocation of Nile River water resources. Diplomatic efforts must focus on fostering dialogue, transparency, and equitable sharing of water, ensuring that the needs of all riparian countries are met.

By acknowledging the significance of agriculture and irrigation in the Nile River basin, diplomats can contribute to the sustainable management of the precious water resources, promote food security, and foster peaceful cooperation among the riparian countries.

Water management practices for sustainable agriculture in the region

Agriculture plays a vital role in the economies of the countries in the Nile River basin. However, the increasing water scarcity in the region poses a significant challenge to sustainable agricultural practices. In this subchapter, we will explore various water management strategies that can be implemented to ensure the long-term sustainability of agriculture in the Nile River basin.

One of the most effective water management practices for sustainable agriculture is the adoption of efficient irrigation techniques. Traditional flood irrigation methods, which are commonly used in the region, result in significant water losses due to evaporation and runoff. By transitioning to modern irrigation systems, such as drip irrigation or sprinkler irrigation, farmers can reduce water wastage and ensure that the water reaches the plant roots more efficiently.

Another important aspect of water management for sustainable agriculture is the implementation of water-saving techniques. This can include the use of mulching, which helps retain soil moisture, and the adoption of crop rotation and cover cropping practices, which improve soil health and reduce water requirements. Furthermore, the use of precision farming techniques, such as remote sensing and data analytics, can help farmers optimize their water usage by providing real-time information about soil moisture levels and crop water requirements.

In addition to on-farm water management practices, policymakers and international organizations can play a crucial role in promoting sustainable agriculture in the region. This can be achieved through the development and enforcement of water allocation policies that prioritize the needs of agriculture while ensuring the conservation of water resources. Furthermore, investments in infrastructure, such as water storage facilities and irrigation networks, can help improve water availability for agricultural purposes.

It is also important to consider the impacts of climate change on water availability in the Nile River basin. As temperatures rise and rainfall patterns become more unpredictable, farmers will face even greater challenges in managing water resources. Therefore, it is crucial to promote climate-smart agricultural practices that are resilient to climate change and minimize water usage.

In conclusion, sustainable agriculture in the Nile River basin requires the implementation of effective water management practices. By adopting efficient irrigation techniques, promoting water-saving techniques, and investing in infrastructure, policymakers and farmers can ensure the long-term viability of agriculture in the region. Moreover, considering the impacts of climate change and promoting climate-smart agricultural practices are essential for adapting to future water scarcity challenges.

Innovative approaches to improve water efficiency in agricultural practices

Agriculture is a vital sector in the Nile River basin, providing food security and livelihoods for millions of people. However, it is also a major consumer of water resources, putting increased pressure on an already scarce resource. To address this challenge, innovative approaches are needed to improve water efficiency in agricultural practices.

One such approach is the adoption of precision agriculture techniques. Precision agriculture involves the use of advanced technologies, such as remote sensing and Geographic Information Systems (GIS), to optimize the use of water and other inputs in farming. By precisely mapping soil moisture levels and crop water requirements, farmers can apply water only where and when it is needed, reducing wastage and increasing efficiency. This approach has been proven effective in reducing water use in various crops, including maize, wheat, and vegetables.

Another innovative approach is the use of drought-tolerant and water-efficient crop varieties. Plant breeding programs have developed crop varieties that require less water without compromising yield. These varieties have been successfully introduced in some parts of the Nile River basin, helping farmers cope with water scarcity. Additionally, the use of mulching and cover crops can help reduce evaporation and improve soil moisture retention, further enhancing water efficiency in agriculture.

Furthermore, the promotion of alternative irrigation methods can significantly improve water efficiency. Traditional flood irrigation methods result in significant water losses due to evaporation and runoff.

Switching to more efficient irrigation techniques, such as drip irrigation or sprinkler systems, can save water by delivering it directly to the plant roots and minimizing losses. These methods also allow for precise control of water application, reducing overwatering and nutrient leaching.

In addition to technological innovations, innovative approaches to water management in agriculture also involve policy and institutional reforms. Integrated water resources management, which aims to coordinate water allocation and use across different sectors, can help optimize water use in agriculture. This requires effective governance mechanisms, stakeholder participation, and the establishment of water rights and allocation systems that incentivize water efficiency.

By adopting these innovative approaches to improve water efficiency in agricultural practices, the Nile River basin can ensure sustainable water use for agriculture while safeguarding the availability of water for other sectors and future generations. Diplomats and policymakers play a crucial role in promoting and supporting these approaches through international cooperation, knowledge sharing, and the establishment of effective water governance frameworks in the Nile River basin.

Chapter 8: Urbanization and water pollution in the Nile River: Implications and mitigation measures

Urbanization trends and their impact on water resources in the Nile River basin

Urbanization is a global phenomenon that has significant implications for water resources. In the context of the Nile River basin, the rapid urbanization occurring in the region is presenting unique challenges for water management. This subchapter explores the urbanization trends in the Nile River basin and their impact on water resources, addressing the concerns of diplomats and the niches interested in the precious water of the Nile River.

The Nile River basin is home to several rapidly growing cities, such as Cairo, Khartoum, and Addis Ababa. These urban centers are experiencing population growth, increased industrialization, and changing lifestyles, all of which contribute to a growing demand for water. As more people migrate to urban areas, the strain on water resources intensifies, resulting in increased water scarcity and pollution.

The expansion of urban areas leads to the encroachment on natural water bodies, wetlands, and floodplains, which are essential for maintaining the ecological balance and the sustainability of water resources. Urban development often involves the construction of infrastructure such as roads, buildings, and sewage systems, which can disrupt the natural hydrological cycle and contribute to water pollution.

Furthermore, urban centers generate large volumes of wastewater, which, if not properly treated, can contaminate water bodies and groundwater sources. Inadequate sanitation systems and waste management practices further exacerbate the pollution of the Nile River.

Addressing the challenges posed by urbanization requires a multi-faceted approach. Diplomats and stakeholders need to collaborate to develop integrated water management strategies that take into account the needs of both urban and rural areas. This includes investing in infrastructure for water supply, sanitation, and wastewater treatment, as well as promoting water conservation and efficiency measures.

Additionally, it is crucial to raise awareness among urban populations about the importance of responsible water use and pollution prevention. Public participation and engagement in decision-making processes can foster a sense of ownership and responsibility, leading to more sustainable water management practices.

In conclusion, the rapid urbanization occurring in the Nile River basin has significant implications for water resources. The growing urban centers are placing increasing pressure on water availability and quality. Addressing these challenges requires a collaborative and integrated approach, involving diplomats, international organizations, and local communities. By implementing sustainable water management strategies and promoting responsible urban development, it is possible to mitigate the negative impacts of urbanization on the precious water resources of the Nile River.

Water pollution sources and consequences for human health and ecosystems

Water pollution is a pressing issue that poses significant threats to both human health and the delicate ecosystems of the Nile River basin. This subchapter aims to provide diplomats with a comprehensive understanding of the sources of water pollution in the Nile River and the consequences it has on human health and the environment.

The Nile River, known as the lifeblood of Egypt and several other countries in the basin, faces numerous challenges when it comes to water pollution. The sources of pollution are diverse and include industrial discharges, agricultural runoff, sewage, and improper waste disposal. These pollutants find their way into the river through various channels, leading to the contamination of water resources.

The consequences of water pollution for human health are grave. The consumption of contaminated water can result in waterborne diseases such as cholera, typhoid, and dysentery. The lack of clean drinking water has a disproportionate impact on vulnerable populations, exacerbating health inequalities. Additionally, polluted water affects the availability of safe water for irrigation and agricultural purposes, jeopardizing food security in the region.

The Nile River's delicate ecosystems also suffer from water pollution. The discharge of industrial and agricultural chemicals, as well as untreated sewage, leads to the eutrophication of water bodies and the destruction of aquatic habitats. This poses a threat to the biodiversity of the river, affecting fish populations and other aquatic organisms. Furthermore, the pollution can have cascading effects on the entire ecosystem, disrupting the balance of the Nile River basin.

To mitigate the consequences of water pollution, a multi-faceted approach is required. Diplomats need to prioritize the implementation of effective pollution control measures, such as the regulation of industrial discharges and the treatment of wastewater. Collaborative efforts among countries in the Nile River basin are crucial to address shared challenges and develop sustainable solutions.

Furthermore, raising awareness among the public about the importance of water conservation and proper waste management is essential. Encouraging the adoption of eco-friendly practices and supporting the development of innovative technologies for water treatment can also contribute to mitigating water pollution in the Nile River.

By understanding the sources and consequences of water pollution in the Nile River, diplomats can play a crucial role in advocating for policies and initiatives that prioritize the protection and sustainable management of this precious resource. Only through collaborative efforts and informed decision-making can we ensure the availability of clean water for present and future generations in the Nile River basin.

Strategies for mitigating urban water pollution and promoting sustainable urban development

Urbanization and rapid population growth have led to increased water pollution in the Nile River and its tributaries. As cities expand and industries flourish, the need for effective strategies to mitigate water pollution and promote sustainable urban development becomes imperative. This subchapter explores various measures and approaches that can be taken to address these challenges.

One of the key strategies for mitigating urban water pollution is the implementation of robust wastewater treatment systems. Diplomats and international organizations can collaborate with governments to invest in modern treatment facilities that can effectively remove pollutants and contaminants from wastewater before it is released back into the river. This will not only help in reducing water pollution but also ensure the availability of clean water for various purposes.

Another important aspect is the promotion of sustainable urban development practices. Diplomats can advocate for the adoption of green infrastructure initiatives such as rainwater harvesting, permeable pavements, and green roofs. These practices can help in reducing the burden on the water supply by promoting the use of alternative water sources and reducing stormwater runoff, which often carries pollutants into the river.

Furthermore, raising awareness among the population about the importance of water conservation and pollution prevention is crucial. Diplomats can engage with local communities, organize workshops, and implement educational campaigns to encourage responsible water usage and waste management practices. By promoting behavioral change, diplomats can contribute to long-term sustainable water management.

Collaboration between countries sharing the Nile River basin is also essential in addressing urban water pollution. Diplomatic efforts can focus on fostering cooperation and developing joint strategies to tackle pollution hotspots and industrial discharges. Bilateral or multilateral agreements can be established to regulate the discharge of pollutants into the river, enforce strict environmental standards, and ensure compliance through monitoring and reporting mechanisms.

Furthermore, the use of innovative technologies and approaches can play a significant role in sustainable water management. Diplomats can support research and development initiatives to identify and implement innovative solutions such as advanced water treatment technologies, smart water management systems, and real-time monitoring tools. These technologies can help in improving water quality, reducing wastage, and enhancing overall efficiency in water use.

In conclusion, mitigating urban water pollution and promoting sustainable urban development in the Nile River basin require a combination of strategies and collaborations. Diplomats can play a pivotal role in advocating for and implementing robust wastewater treatment systems, promoting sustainable urban development practices, raising awareness, fostering international cooperation, and supporting the adoption of innovative technologies. By adopting a holistic approach, we can ensure the preservation of the precious water resources of the Nile River for future generations and foster sustainable development in the region.

Chapter 9: The role of dams and reservoirs in managing Nile River water resources

Benefits and challenges of dam construction in the Nile River basin

Dams have been widely used in the Nile River basin to manage water resources and address various challenges. While they offer significant benefits, they also come with certain challenges that need to be considered. This subchapter explores the benefits and challenges of dam construction in the Nile River basin, providing valuable insights for diplomats and those interested in water scarcity diplomacy.

One of the primary benefits of dam construction is the regulation of water flow. Dams can store water during periods of high rainfall and release it during dry seasons, ensuring a consistent water supply for various purposes such as irrigation, domestic use, and hydropower generation. This water regulation helps mitigate the effects of water scarcity and reduces the vulnerability of communities to droughts and floods.

Furthermore, dams provide a renewable and clean source of energy through hydropower generation. The Nile River basin has immense potential for hydropower, and dam construction can harness this energy, reducing dependence on fossil fuels and contributing to sustainable development. Hydropower can also be a source of revenue for countries, as excess energy can be sold to neighboring regions.

However, dam construction also presents several challenges. One of the main concerns is the displacement of communities living in the dam's vicinity. Reservoirs created by dams often require the relocation of people, which can lead to social, economic, and cultural disruptions. Diplomats need to address these challenges by ensuring proper compensation, resettlement, and livelihood restoration for affected communities.

Another challenge is the impact on the environment and ecosystems. Dams can alter the natural flow of the river, affecting the migration patterns of fish, sediment transport, and overall ecological balance. Diplomats must consider environmental impact assessments and implement mitigation measures to minimize these effects and preserve the biodiversity of the Nile River basin.

Lastly, dam construction can also lead to transboundary conflicts over water allocation. The Nile River basin is shared by multiple countries, and the construction of dams can affect downstream nations. Diplomats play a crucial role in facilitating dialogue, negotiation, and cooperation to address these disputes and ensure fair and equitable sharing of water resources.

In conclusion, dam construction in the Nile River basin offers numerous benefits, including water regulation and hydropower generation. However, it also poses challenges such as community displacement, environmental impacts, and transboundary conflicts. Diplomats need to engage in water scarcity diplomacy and work collaboratively to address these challenges, ensuring sustainable and equitable management of Nile River water resources.

Impacts of dams on water availability, ecosystems, and downstream communities

Dams play a significant role in managing water resources, particularly in the context of the Nile River Basin. However, their construction and operation can have profound impacts on water availability, ecosystems, and downstream communities. This subchapter explores these impacts, shedding light on the challenges and potential solutions associated with dams in the region.

One of the primary impacts of dams is on water availability. While dams can provide a reliable water supply for various purposes such as irrigation, hydropower generation, and domestic use, they also have the potential to alter the natural flow of the river. This alteration can lead to reduced downstream water availability, affecting ecosystems and communities dependent on the river for their water needs. Diplomats need to understand these dynamics to effectively address disputes and challenges related to water scarcity in the Nile River Basin.

The construction of dams can also have adverse effects on ecosystems. Dams can disrupt the natural flow of the river, affecting the habitats of fish and other aquatic species. Furthermore, the creation of reservoirs behind the dams can lead to the submergence of large areas of land, resulting in the loss of valuable ecosystems and displacement of local communities. Diplomats must consider the ecological impacts of dams and work towards mitigating them through sustainable management practices.

Downstream communities are particularly vulnerable to the impacts of dams. Reduced water availability and changes in the river's flow can have severe consequences for agriculture, livelihoods, and access to clean water. Diplomats need to engage with these communities, understanding their perspectives and concerns, and ensure their voices are heard in decision-making processes.

Mitigation measures and potential solutions to address the impacts of dams on water availability, ecosystems, and downstream communities are crucial. Diplomats can play a pivotal role in promoting sustainable management practices, ensuring the equitable distribution of water resources, and fostering dialogue and cooperation among riparian countries.

In conclusion, the impacts of dams on water availability, ecosystems, and downstream communities in the Nile River Basin are significant.

Diplomats must understand these impacts and work towards sustainable management practices, taking into account the perspectives of indigenous communities, the needs of downstream communities, and the ecological integrity of the river system. By addressing these challenges, diplomats can contribute to resolving water disputes and ensuring the long-term availability of the precious water resources of the Nile River.

Integrated water management approaches for dam operations and water allocation

In the Nile River Basin, where water scarcity is a pressing issue, it is crucial to adopt integrated water management approaches for dam operations and water allocation. This subchapter aims to provide diplomats with insights into the challenges and potential solutions associated with managing the precious water of the Nile River.

One of the main causes of water scarcity in the Nile River Basin is the historical and ongoing disputes over the allocation of water resources. These disputes have often led to tensions between riparian countries, making it essential for diplomats to understand the hydropolitics involved and the role international organizations play in resolving such disputes.

Furthermore, the impact of climate change on the availability of Nile River water cannot be ignored. As temperatures rise and rainfall patterns become unpredictable, it is imperative to develop adaptive strategies for managing water resources. Diplomats need to be aware of the potential consequences of climate change on water availability and work towards implementing sustainable measures to mitigate its effects.

Population growth and urbanization also pose significant challenges to water management in the Nile River Basin. The increasing demand for water, particularly for agriculture and domestic use, necessitates innovative approaches to ensure water security. Diplomats should explore strategies that promote efficient water use and conservation, in addition to addressing the issue of water pollution resulting from urbanization.

Dams and reservoirs play a crucial role in managing water resources in the Nile River Basin. Diplomats need to understand the benefits and challenges associated with dam operations, such as the potential impacts on downstream communities and ecosystems. Integrated approaches that consider the needs of all stakeholders and ensure equitable water allocation are essential for sustainable dam operations.

Indigenous communities in the Nile River Basin have their unique perspectives on the use and conservation of water resources. Diplomats should engage with these communities and incorporate their traditional knowledge into water management strategies. Such collaboration can contribute to more inclusive and sustainable approaches.

Finally, innovative technologies and approaches can play a significant role in the sustainable management of the Nile River water. Diplomats should explore and promote the adoption of technologies that enhance water efficiency, such as drip irrigation and desalination. Additionally, they should advocate for the implementation of integrated water management systems that consider the interconnectedness of water resources and ecosystems.

In conclusion, integrated water management approaches are vital for dam operations and water allocation in the Nile River Basin. Diplomats have a crucial role to play in addressing the challenges associated with water scarcity and resolving disputes over water resources. By considering the perspectives of various stakeholders, adopting innovative technologies, and promoting sustainable practices, diplomats can contribute to the effective and equitable management of the precious water of the Nile River.

Chapter 10: Indigenous communities' perspectives on the use and conservation of Nile River water

Cultural significance of the Nile River for indigenous communities

The Nile River holds immense cultural significance for the indigenous communities living in its basin. For generations, these communities have relied on the river for their livelihoods, cultural practices, and spiritual beliefs. This subchapter explores the deep-rooted cultural connections between indigenous communities and the Nile River, shedding light on the importance of understanding and respecting these traditions when addressing water scarcity challenges in the region.

Indigenous communities have a profound respect for the Nile River, considering it a sacred entity that sustains their way of life. The river is often personified as a deity, revered for its life-giving properties. Rituals and ceremonies are conducted to pay homage to the river, seeking its blessings and protection. These practices serve as a reminder of the close relationship between indigenous communities and the Nile River, and the inherent responsibility to preserve its integrity.

The Nile River's cultural significance extends beyond spiritual beliefs. Indigenous communities have developed unique practices and knowledge systems related to water management. Traditional methods of irrigation, water storage, and conservation have been passed down through generations, ensuring the sustainable use of water resources. These traditional water management strategies, rooted in indigenous knowledge, can offer valuable insights for modern water scarcity diplomacy in the Nile River basin.

Furthermore, the Nile River plays a central role in the cultural identity and heritage of indigenous communities. It has inspired art, music, folklore, and oral traditions that celebrate the river's importance in their lives. Indigenous communities have developed intricate systems of storytelling, using the river as a metaphor for life's journey and the interconnectedness of all beings. Preserving and promoting these cultural expressions is crucial for maintaining the unique identity of indigenous communities in the face of increasing water scarcity challenges.

Diplomats and international organizations involved in addressing water scarcity in the Nile River basin must recognize and respect the cultural significance of the river for indigenous communities. By incorporating indigenous perspectives and knowledge into water management strategies, a more holistic and sustainable approach can be achieved. This subchapter emphasizes the need for inclusive and culturally sensitive policies that empower indigenous communities as custodians of the Nile River's cultural heritage and guardians of its scarce water resources.

In conclusion, the cultural significance of the Nile River for indigenous communities cannot be overstated. Recognizing and respecting the deep connections between indigenous communities and the river is crucial for effective water scarcity diplomacy in the region. By understanding and incorporating indigenous perspectives and knowledge, diplomats can work towards sustainable solutions that preserve both the cultural heritage and the precious water resources of the Nile River.

Indigenous knowledge and practices for water conservation and sustainability

Water scarcity is a pressing issue in the Nile River Basin, and addressing this challenge requires a comprehensive understanding of the region's unique context. One crucial aspect often overlooked is the wealth of indigenous knowledge and practices that have sustained local communities for centuries. This subchapter explores the invaluable insights offered by indigenous communities in the realm of water conservation and sustainability.

Indigenous communities living along the Nile River have developed intricate systems to manage water resources effectively. Drawing on generations of experience, they have cultivated an intimate understanding of the river's ebb and flow, its seasonal variations, and the delicate balance between human needs and ecological preservation. These communities have harnessed this knowledge to develop innovative practices that ensure the sustainable use of Nile River water.

One such practice is the use of traditional irrigation methods that maximize water efficiency. Indigenous farmers have perfected techniques like furrow irrigation and flood recession agriculture, which minimize water loss through evaporation and ensure optimal distribution across fields. These methods not only optimize water utilization but also promote soil fertility and reduce the risk of salinization.

Furthermore, indigenous communities have a deep respect for the interconnectedness of the Nile River ecosystem. They have long recognized the importance of protecting riverine habitats and maintaining the health of the river's tributaries. By conserving forests, wetlands, and other critical ecosystems, these communities safeguard the water sources that sustain their livelihoods and preserve biodiversity.

In addition to their traditional practices, indigenous communities have valuable knowledge about sustainable water management in times of scarcity. They possess a wealth of wisdom on rainwater harvesting, water storage, and the construction of small-scale reservoirs. These techniques enable communities to store water during periods of abundance and access it during dry seasons, ensuring their resilience in the face of water scarcity.

Recognizing and incorporating indigenous knowledge and practices into water management policies is crucial for sustainable development in the Nile River Basin. Diplomats and policymakers must engage with indigenous communities, acknowledging their expertise and involving them in decision-making processes. This will not only foster cultural preservation but also enhance the effectiveness of water conservation efforts.

In conclusion, indigenous knowledge and practices offer valuable insights into water conservation and sustainability in the Nile River Basin. By understanding and incorporating these practices, diplomats and stakeholders can develop more comprehensive and effective strategies for managing water scarcity. Engaging with indigenous communities will not only improve water resource management but also promote cultural diversity and social equity in the region.

Importance of including indigenous perspectives in water management decisions

In recent years, there has been a growing recognition of the importance of including indigenous perspectives in water management decisions. This shift in approach is crucial, especially when it comes to the management of the precious water resources of the Nile River Basin. Diplomats and policymakers involved in the negotiation and decision-making processes of water scarcity diplomacy in the Nile River Basin must understand the value of including indigenous communities' perspectives in these discussions.

Indigenous communities have a deep-rooted connection to the land and water resources of the Nile River Basin. Their traditional knowledge, practices, and cultural values are directly linked to sustainable water management. By excluding indigenous perspectives from decision-making processes, we risk overlooking crucial insights and potential solutions that can contribute to the sustainable management of the Nile River water resources.

Indigenous communities have a unique understanding of the local ecosystems and the intricate interplay between water availability, climate change, and natural resource management. Their perspectives can provide valuable insights into the causes and effects of water scarcity in the Nile River Basin. By incorporating their knowledge, we can develop more effective strategies to address the challenges posed by climate change and population growth.

Furthermore, historical and ongoing disputes over the allocation of Nile River water resources can benefit from indigenous perspectives. Indigenous communities often hold ancestral rights and traditional water management practices that have been honed over generations. Their involvement in the negotiation and resolution of these disputes can help foster a sense of ownership, ensuring that decisions are equitable and sustainable for all stakeholders involved.

Including indigenous perspectives also contributes to the broader goal of promoting social justice and equality. Indigenous communities are often marginalized and have limited access to decision-making processes. By actively involving them in water management decisions, we can work towards empowering these communities and ensuring that their rights and interests are respected.

In conclusion, the inclusion of indigenous perspectives in water management decisions is of utmost importance. Diplomats and policymakers involved in water scarcity diplomacy in the Nile River Basin must recognize the value of indigenous knowledge and practices. By doing so, we can foster more sustainable and equitable approaches to the management of the precious water resources of the Nile River.

Chapter 11: Innovative technologies and approaches for sustainable management of the Nile River water

Emerging technologies for water conservation and efficient water use

In recent years, emerging technologies have played a crucial role in addressing the challenges of water scarcity and promoting efficient water use in the Nile River basin. These innovative solutions have the potential to revolutionize water management practices, ensuring sustainable access to the precious water resources of the Nile River. This subchapter explores some of the most promising technologies and approaches that can contribute to the sustainable management of Nile River water.

One such technology is the use of advanced sensors and monitoring systems. These devices enable real-time data collection on water quality, quantity, and usage, providing policymakers and water managers with valuable insights for decision-making. For instance, remote sensing technologies can detect changes in vegetation patterns, allowing for more efficient irrigation practices and reducing water wastage in agriculture.

Another emerging technology is the application of artificial intelligence (AI) and machine learning algorithms in water management. By analyzing large datasets, AI systems can predict water demand, identify leakages in water infrastructure, and optimize water allocation. These intelligent systems can also support policymakers in developing effective water conservation policies and strategies.

Furthermore, the adoption of smart metering devices can enable individuals and households to monitor their water consumption in real-time. Coupled with mobile applications, these devices empower users to make informed decisions about their water usage, promoting behavioral change towards more sustainable practices.

In addition, innovative water treatment technologies have the potential to alleviate the challenges of water pollution in the Nile River. Advanced filtration systems, such as reverse osmosis and ultraviolet disinfection, can effectively remove contaminants and ensure the provision of safe drinking water. Moreover, decentralized wastewater treatment systems can recycle and reuse water, reducing the strain on freshwater resources.

Lastly, the development of desalination technologies holds promise for increasing water supply in the Nile River basin. Desalination involves the removal of salt and impurities from seawater or brackish water, providing an alternative source of freshwater. Although desalination is energy-intensive and expensive, ongoing research aims to make this technology more affordable and sustainable.

As the demand for water continues to rise, it is crucial for diplomats and international organizations to embrace these emerging technologies and promote their adoption in the Nile River basin. By harnessing the power of innovation, stakeholders can work towards a future where water scarcity is mitigated, and the precious water resources of the Nile River are managed efficiently and sustainably.

Sustainable water management practices in the Nile River basin

The Nile River is not only a vital source of water but also a symbol of life and prosperity for the communities residing within its basin. However, the increasing population, climate change, and ongoing disputes over water allocation pose significant challenges to the sustainable management of this precious resource. This subchapter aims to provide valuable insights to diplomats and various stakeholders within the Nile River basin on sustainable water management practices that can help address these challenges.

One of the key causes of water scarcity in the Nile River basin is the increasing demand due to population growth. As the population continues to rise, the demand for water for agriculture, industrial, and domestic purposes also increases. To manage this demand, it is crucial to promote efficient water use practices such as drip irrigation, water recycling, and rainwater harvesting. These practices can help reduce water wastage and ensure that limited water resources are utilized optimally.

Another important aspect of sustainable water management in the Nile River basin is addressing the impacts of climate change. Climate change has led to unpredictable rainfall patterns and increased evaporation rates, resulting in reduced water availability. Diplomats and stakeholders should prioritize the development and implementation of climate change adaptation strategies such as water storage systems, watershed management, and reforestation programs. These measures can help mitigate the effects of climate change and enhance the resilience of communities dependent on the Nile River.

Furthermore, resolving historical and ongoing disputes over water allocation is crucial for sustainable water management. Diplomats and international organizations play a pivotal role in facilitating negotiations and mediating conflicts among riparian countries. Collaborative agreements, such as the Nile Basin Initiative, can help establish frameworks for equitable water sharing and strengthen cooperation among nations.

The subchapter also delves into the role of dams and reservoirs in managing Nile River water resources. While these infrastructures provide opportunities for hydropower generation and water storage, they can also have adverse environmental and social impacts. Therefore, it is imperative to implement sustainable dam operations that consider the ecological needs of the river and the livelihoods of communities dependent on it.

Furthermore, the subchapter explores the perspectives of indigenous communities on the use and conservation of Nile River water. Their traditional knowledge and practices can offer valuable insights into sustainable water management approaches that prioritize the long-term well-being of the river and its surrounding ecosystem.

Lastly, innovative technologies and approaches for sustainable water management are discussed. These include the use of satellite technology for monitoring water resources, desalination techniques, and the promotion of water-efficient crops. By embracing these innovations, diplomats and stakeholders can enhance the efficiency and effectiveness of water management practices in the Nile River basin.

In conclusion, sustainable water management in the Nile River basin is a complex and multidimensional challenge. By adopting efficient water use practices, addressing the impacts of climate change, resolving water disputes, considering the perspectives of indigenous communities, and embracing innovative technologies, diplomats and stakeholders can contribute to the long-term sustainability of this vital resource.

Collaborative initiatives and partnerships for implementing innovative water solutions

Water scarcity in the Nile River basin poses significant challenges that require collaborative efforts and innovative solutions. Diplomats and various stakeholders play a crucial role in addressing these challenges and finding potential solutions. This subchapter explores the importance of collaborative initiatives and partnerships in implementing innovative water solutions in the Nile River basin.

Collaboration at the regional, national, and international levels is essential for effective water management in the Nile River basin.

Diplomats can facilitate dialogue and negotiations between riparian countries to resolve disputes and allocate water resources equitably. They can also advocate for the importance of water cooperation and encourage the establishment of joint institutions for managing the Nile River water.

Partnerships between governments, non-governmental organizations (NGOs), and the private sector are key to implementing innovative water solutions. Diplomats can foster these partnerships by facilitating cooperation and knowledge-sharing among stakeholders. They can encourage governments to collaborate with NGOs and the private sector in developing and implementing water management projects.

International organizations also play a critical role in resolving Nile River water disputes and promoting sustainable water management. Diplomats can work closely with these organizations, such as the United Nations and regional bodies like the Nile Basin Initiative, to support their efforts in addressing water scarcity challenges. They can advocate for increased funding for water-related projects and help coordinate the activities of various stakeholders.

Innovative technologies and approaches are vital for sustainable water management in the Nile River basin. Diplomats can promote the adoption of these technologies by facilitating technology transfers and providing financial and technical support. They can also encourage research and development in water-related fields to foster innovation and find new solutions to address water scarcity.

Collaborative initiatives and partnerships are essential for implementing innovative water solutions in the Nile River basin. Diplomats can play a crucial role in facilitating cooperation, advocating for sustainable water management, and supporting the efforts of various stakeholders. By working together, we can address the challenges of water scarcity and ensure the availability of precious Nile River water for present and future generations.

Conclusion: Toward Sustainable Water Diplomacy in the Nile River Basin

Recap of key challenges and potential solutions

In this subchapter, we will provide a recap of the key challenges faced in the Nile River Basin and potential solutions to address them. As diplomats, it is crucial to understand the complexity of the issues and explore possible avenues for cooperation among the riparian countries.

One of the primary challenges we discussed is the disputes and historical conflicts over the allocation of Nile River water resources. The Nile River is a lifeline for many countries, and the equitable distribution of water is of vital importance. Potential solutions could include the establishment of a legal framework or a cooperative agreement between the riparian countries to ensure fair and sustainable water allocation.

Water scarcity in the Nile River basin is another critical challenge. This scarcity is caused by various factors, including population growth, climate change, and inefficient water management practices. To address this issue, a multi-faceted approach is required. This involves promoting water conservation measures, implementing efficient irrigation techniques, and investing in infrastructure for rainwater harvesting and storage.

The impact of climate change on the availability of Nile River water cannot be ignored. Rising temperatures and changing rainfall patterns pose a significant threat to the region's water resources. Diplomats can advocate for international cooperation in reducing greenhouse gas emissions and support initiatives aimed at adapting to climate change impacts, such as the development of drought-resistant crops and the implementation of climate-resilient infrastructure.

Agricultural challenges are also prevalent in the Nile River basin. Rapid population growth and increased food demand put additional pressure on water resources. Diplomats can encourage the adoption of sustainable agricultural practices, including precision irrigation systems, crop rotation, and agroforestry. Furthermore, promoting research and development in drought-resistant crops can help mitigate the impact of water scarcity on food security.

Urbanization and water pollution are key concerns in the Nile River basin. The rapid growth of cities along the river leads to increased wastewater discharge and pollution. Diplomats can support the development and implementation of wastewater treatment plants, as well as the promotion of public awareness campaigns to reduce water pollution.

The role of dams and reservoirs in managing Nile River water resources is also a topic of concern. Diplomats can facilitate dialogue among riparian countries to establish guidelines for the construction and operation of dams, ensuring that their benefits are maximized while minimizing negative impacts on downstream countries.

Lastly, the subchapter explores indigenous communities' perspectives on the use and conservation of Nile River water. Diplomats can engage with these communities and integrate their traditional knowledge into water management plans, ensuring a holistic and inclusive approach to water governance.

In conclusion, addressing the challenges in the Nile River Basin requires a collaborative and multi-dimensional approach. By understanding the issues at hand and exploring potential solutions, diplomats can play a crucial role in fostering cooperation and sustainable water management among riparian countries.

Importance of diplomatic efforts in addressing water scarcity in the region

Water scarcity is a pressing issue that affects the entire Nile River basin, and it requires a collaborative and diplomatic approach to find sustainable solutions. As diplomats, it is crucial to recognize the significance of diplomatic efforts in addressing water scarcity in the region. This subchapter aims to shed light on the importance of diplomatic initiatives in resolving disputes, managing water resources, and promoting cooperation among riparian states.

The precious water of the Nile River is a source of disputes, challenges, but also potential solutions. Diplomatic efforts play a pivotal role in mediating these conflicts and facilitating dialogue between the concerned parties. By engaging in diplomatic negotiations, diplomats can foster trust, build relationships, and help find mutually beneficial solutions that address the water needs of all riparian states.

One of the key causes of water scarcity in the Nile River basin is climate change. As diplomats, it is essential to understand the impact of climate change on the availability of Nile River water and advocate for climate action. By engaging in international forums and negotiations, diplomats can contribute to the development of policies and agreements that address climate change and its effects on water resources.

Historical and ongoing disputes over the allocation of Nile River water resources require diplomatic intervention. Diplomats can facilitate negotiations, mediate between conflicting parties, and help establish equitable sharing mechanisms that ensure the fair distribution of water resources. Through diplomatic efforts, it is possible to find common ground and resolve long-standing disputes.

International organizations also play a crucial role in resolving Nile River water disputes. Diplomats can collaborate with these organizations to develop frameworks, guidelines, and initiatives that promote cooperation among riparian states. By leveraging the expertise and resources of international organizations, diplomats can enhance the effectiveness of their diplomatic efforts and promote sustainable water management practices.

The impact of population growth on the demand for Nile River water cannot be ignored. Diplomatic efforts should focus on advocating for population control measures, promoting sustainable agricultural practices, and encouraging water conservation strategies. By addressing these challenges, diplomats can mitigate the increasing demand for water resources in the region.

In conclusion, water scarcity in the Nile River basin requires diplomatic efforts to address disputes, manage resources, and promote cooperation. As diplomats, it is crucial to recognize the importance of diplomatic initiatives in resolving conflicts, advocating for climate action, and finding equitable solutions. By engaging in diplomatic negotiations, collaborating with international organizations, and addressing the challenges of population growth, diplomats can contribute to the sustainable management of Nile River water resources and ensure a prosperous future for the region.

Call to action for diplomats to prioritize sustainable water management in the Nile River basin.

Call to Action for Diplomats to Prioritize Sustainable Water Management in the Nile River Basin

The Nile River basin is facing an urgent and escalating water scarcity crisis, which demands immediate attention and action from diplomats. As representatives of their respective nations, diplomats play a crucial role in addressing the challenges posed by water scarcity and ensuring sustainable water management practices in the Nile River basin.

The precious water of the Nile River is at the heart of numerous disputes, challenges, and potential solutions. It is essential for diplomats to recognize the significance of this issue and prioritize it on their diplomatic agenda. By doing so, they can contribute to the resolution of historical and ongoing disputes over the allocation of Nile River water resources.

Climate change exacerbates water scarcity in the Nile River basin, making it imperative for diplomats to advocate for climate action and integrate climate change adaptation strategies into their diplomatic efforts. By understanding the impact of climate change on the availability of Nile River water, diplomats can work towards implementing sustainable water management practices that ensure the long-term availability of this vital resource.

Diplomats should also engage international organizations in resolving Nile River water disputes. By collaborating with organizations such as the United Nations and the African Union, diplomats can facilitate dialogue, negotiation, and the development of cooperative frameworks for water sharing and management.

Furthermore, the growing population in the Nile River basin poses a significant challenge to water resources. Diplomats must recognize the impact of population growth on the demand for Nile River water and promote policies that encourage sustainable water use practices, including efficient irrigation techniques and water conservation measures.

Agricultural challenges in the Nile River basin require innovative water management strategies. Diplomats can support the development and implementation of such strategies, including promoting the use of modern irrigation technologies and encouraging farmers to adopt sustainable agricultural practices.

Urbanization and water pollution in the Nile River also demand the attention of diplomats. They should advocate for stringent regulations to prevent pollution, promote wastewater treatment, and support initiatives that raise awareness about the importance of clean water for both human and ecosystem health.

Diplomats must recognize the crucial role of dams and reservoirs in managing Nile River water resources. By promoting the construction of well-designed and properly managed dams, diplomats can ensure the equitable distribution of water while minimizing environmental impacts.

Indigenous communities' perspectives on the use and conservation of Nile River water should not be overlooked. Diplomats must engage with these communities, respect their traditional knowledge, and involve them in decision-making processes to foster inclusive and sustainable water management practices.

Finally, diplomats should explore and promote innovative technologies and approaches for sustainable management of Nile River water. This includes investing in research and development of desalination technologies, water recycling systems, and efficient water-use practices.

In conclusion, diplomats have a vital role to play in prioritizing sustainable water management in the Nile River basin. By addressing the challenges outlined in this subchapter and taking concrete actions, diplomats can contribute to resolving disputes, mitigating the impact of water scarcity, and ensuring the availability of water resources for present and future generations.